First Facts

Animal Rulers

KINGS OF THE OCEANS

by Jody S. Rake

raintree

a Capstone company — publishers for children

Raintree is an imprint of Capstone Global Library Limited, a company incorporated in England and Wales having its registered office at 264 Banbury Road, Oxford, OX2 7DY – Registered company number: 6695582

www.raintree.co.uk
myorders@raintree.co.uk

Edited by Adrian Vigliano
Designed by Kayla Rossow
Picture research by Kelly Garvin
Production by Kathy McColley
Originated by Captsone Global Library Limited
Printed and bound in China.

ISBN 978 1 4747 4863 6
21 20 19 18 17
10 9 8 7 6 5 4 3 2 1

British Library Cataloguing in Publication Data
A full catalogue record for this book is available from the British Library.

Acknowledgements
We would like to thank the following for permission to reproduce photographs: Minden Pictures/Fred Bavendam, 21; Newscom/Gerard LACZ_VWPics, 7; Shutterstock: Alex Zaitsev, cover (middle), Borisoff, 5, FloridaStock, 15, Gino Santa Maria, cover (top right), 19, Jono Gaza, 11, magnusdeepbelow, 13, Mogens Trolle, 17, nudiblue, cover (top left), Seaphotoart, cover (bottom), wildestanimal, cover (top middle), Willyam Bradberry, 9

Artistic elements: Shutterstock: Airin.dizain, Alemon cz, AlexZaitsev, Ann Doronina, daulon, irabel8, LIORIKI, littlesam, Miceking, Seaphotoart, Vector Tradition SM, white whale, Willyam Bradberry

We would like to thank Jackie Gai for her invaluable help in the preparation of this book.

Every effort has been made to contact copyright holders of material reproduced in this book. Any omissions will be rectified in subsequent printings if notice is given to the publisher.

All the internet addresses (URLs) given in this book were valid at the time of going to press. However, due to the dynamic nature of the internet, some addresses may have changed, or sites may have changed or ceased to exist since publication. While the author and publisher regret any inconvenience this may cause readers, no responsibility for any such changes can be accepted by either the author or the publisher.

Contents

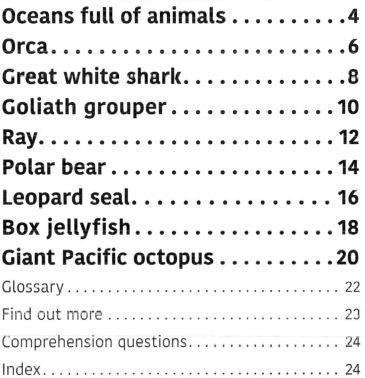

Oceans full of animals

Oceans cover most of Earth's surface. They are wide and deep. Ocean water is salty and full of life. Ocean **food chains** create giant **food webs**. At the top of them are **predators**. They are the rulers of the oceans!

food chain series of plants and animals in which each one in the series eats the one before it

food web many food chains connected to one another

predator animal that hunts other animals for food

Orca

Orcas are **apex** predators. They live in all oceans, but most live closer to the poles. Male orcas can be 5.8 to 6.7 metres (19 to 22 feet) long. But it's not just size that makes orcas amazing. Intelligence and teamwork make orcas great hunters. They feed on fish, squid and seals. But together, a **pod** of orcas can attack a bigger whale!

apex top predator of a food chain
pod group of whales

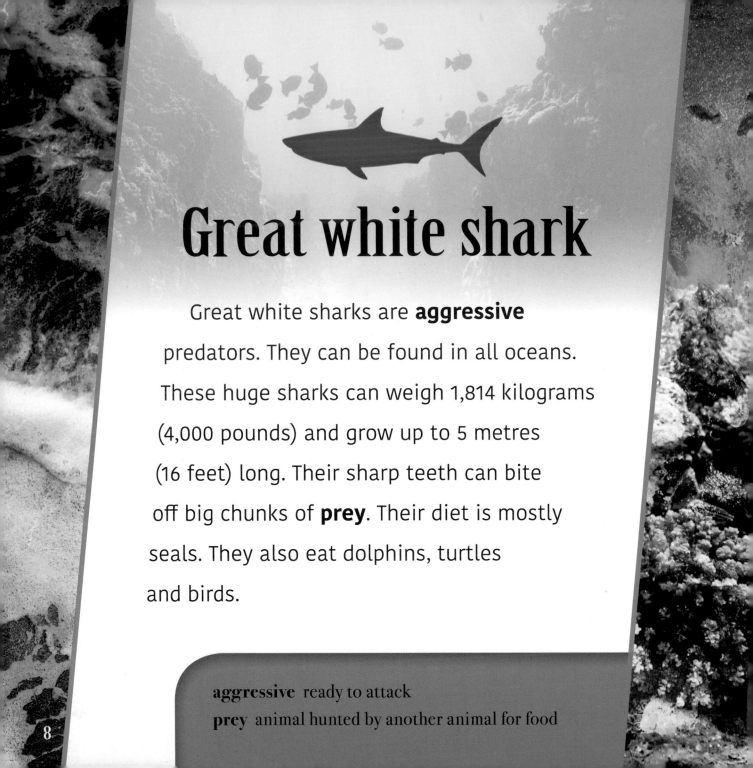

Great white shark

Great white sharks are **aggressive** predators. They can be found in all oceans. These huge sharks can weigh 1,814 kilograms (4,000 pounds) and grow up to 5 metres (16 feet) long. Their sharp teeth can bite off big chunks of **prey**. Their diet is mostly seals. They also eat dolphins, turtles and birds.

aggressive ready to attack
prey animal hunted by another animal for food

Fact! Shark attacks on humans are rare. There are only about 35 attacks each year.

Goliath grouper

Goliath groupers are sea giants.
They live in the Atlantic Ocean. These
fish grow up to 2.4 metres (8 feet) long
and weigh 363 kilograms (800 pounds).
Goliath groupers eat almost any prey
that will fit in their huge mouths. Their
prey includes fish, lobsters, octopuses
and turtles.

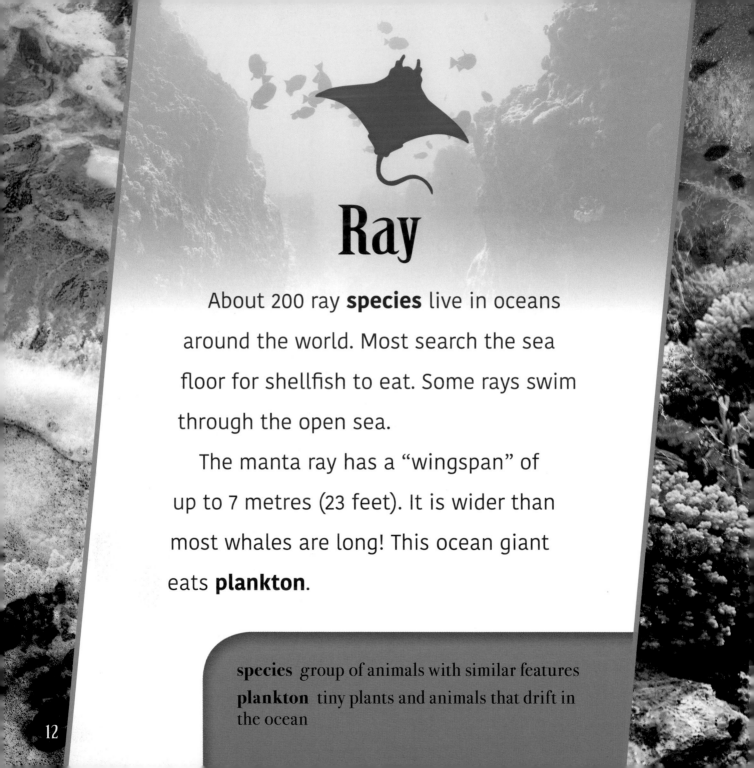

Ray

About 200 ray **species** live in oceans around the world. Most search the sea floor for shellfish to eat. Some rays swim through the open sea.

The manta ray has a "wingspan" of up to 7 metres (23 feet). It is wider than most whales are long! This ocean giant eats **plankton**.

species group of animals with similar features
plankton tiny plants and animals that drift in the ocean

Polar bear

Polar bears are top Arctic predators. They depend on the ocean for food. Much of the Arctic Ocean has a frozen surface for most of the year. Arctic seals swim under the ice. Polar bears hunt seals from above the ice. They wait for seals to come up for air. Polar bears may swim many kilometres in search of places to hunt.

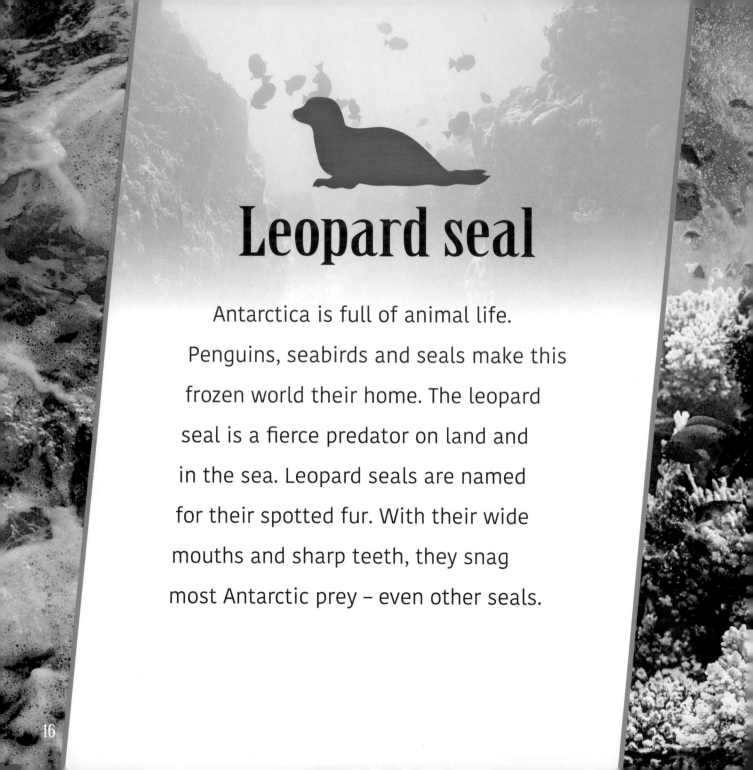

Leopard seal

Antarctica is full of animal life. Penguins, seabirds and seals make this frozen world their home. The leopard seal is a fierce predator on land and in the sea. Leopard seals are named for their spotted fur. With their wide mouths and sharp teeth, they snag most Antarctic prey – even other seals.

Fact! The leopard seal is the only seal that eats other warm-blooded prey.

Box jellyfish

All jellyfish have stinging **tentacles**. But no jellyfish is as feared as the box jellyfish of the Pacific Ocean. Their tentacles are 3 metres (10 feet) and have lots of stingers. Each stinger contains powerful **venom** that stuns or kills prey. Box jellyfish use their stingers to hunt fish and shrimp.

tentacle long, flexible limb used for moving, feeling and grabbing

venom poisonous liquid made by an animal to kill its prey

Fact! The box jellyfish is one of the most dangerous animals on Earth. Its sting can make a human go into shock and drown.

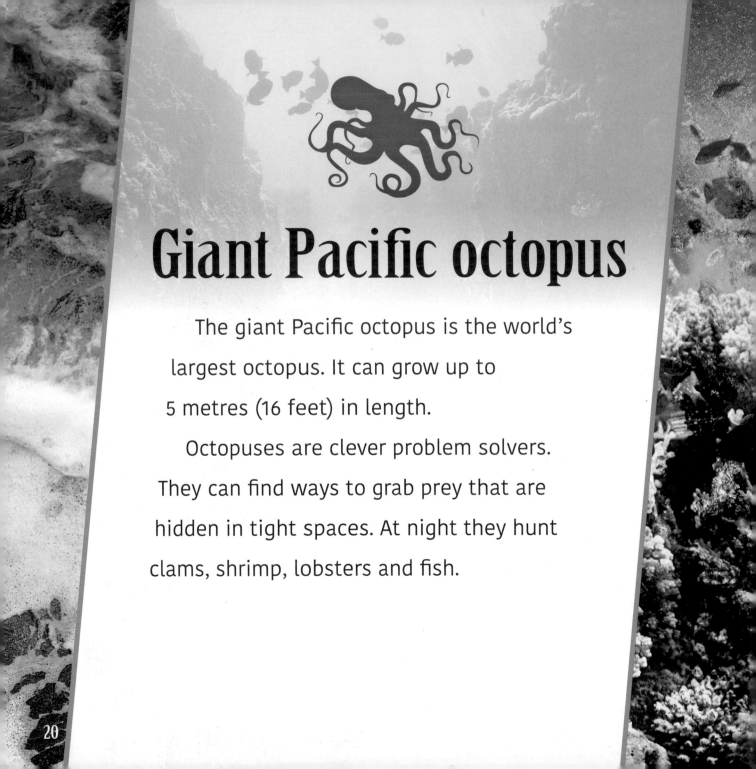

Giant Pacific octopus

The giant Pacific octopus is the world's largest octopus. It can grow up to 5 metres (16 feet) in length.

Octopuses are clever problem solvers. They can find ways to grab prey that are hidden in tight spaces. At night they hunt clams, shrimp, lobsters and fish.

Fact! This type of octopus can change its skin colour to blend into its surroundings.

Glossary

aggressive ready to attack

apex top predator of a food chain

food chain series of plants and animals in which each one in the series eats the one before it

food web many food chains connected to one another

plankton tiny plants and animals that drift in the ocean

pod group of whales

predator animal that hunts other animals for food

prey animal hunted by another animal for food

species group of animals with similar features

tentacle long, flexible limb used for moving, feeling and grabbing

venom poisonous liquid made by an animal to kill its prey

Find out more

Books

It's All About... Snappy Sharks (Kingfisher, 2015)

Killer Whales: Built for the Hunt (Predator Profiles), Christine Zuchora-Walske (Raintree, 2016)

Polar Bears (Animals are Amazing), Valerie Dodden (Franklin Watts, 2014)

Websites

www.dkfindout.com/uk/animals-and-nature/jellyfish-corals-and-anemones/box-jellyfish
Discover more about the box jellyfish on this website.

gowild.wwf.org.uk/regions/polar-fact-files/polar-bear
On this website you can learn about polar bears and even listen to one roar!

Comprehension questions

1. How are oceans different from land? List two things.

2. Study the picture of the grouper on page 11. Then study the picture of the ray on page 13. What similarities do these animals have? How are they different?

3. What would happen if any one of these large predators were to die out? How would their disappearance affect the habitat?

4. The box jellyfish is the most venomous marine animal in the world. What is venom? Hint: Use the glossary for help!

Index